Gods of Greek
Mythology

Other Titles in the *Exploring
Greek Mythology* series include:

Gods of Greek Mythology

Don Nardo

San Diego, CA

© 2020 ReferencePoint Press, Inc.
Printed in the United States

For more information, contact:
ReferencePoint Press, Inc.
PO Box 27779
San Diego, CA 92198
www.ReferencePointPress.com

LIBRARY OF CONGRESS CATALOGING-IN-PUBLICATION DATA

Name: Nardo, Don, 1947– author.
Title: Gods of Greek Mythology/by Don Nardo.
Description: San Diego: ReferencePoint Press, 2019. | Series: Exploring
    Greek Mythology | Includes bibliographical references and index.
Identifiers: LCCN 2018033793 (print) | LCCN 2018035695 (ebook) | ISBN
    9781682826225 (eBook) | ISBN 9781682826218 (hardback)
Subjects: LCSH: Gods, Greek.
Classification: LCC BL783 (ebook) | LCC BL783 .N37 2019 (print) | DDC
    398.20938/01—dc23
LC record available at https://lccn.loc.gov/2018033793

Contents

Introduction

The Ideal of What Humans Should Be and Do

Greek mythology consists of a corpus, or collection, of many hundreds of tales that were central to classical Greek culture. Strictly speaking, modern historians define Greece's Classical Age as the period running from about 500 to the late 300s BCE, when ancient Greek civilization reached its cultural zenith. But in a more general sense, the inhabitants of Greece from around 750 to 300 BCE, who inherited the myths from an earlier era, are often referred to as the classical Greeks. They called that archaic era the Age of Heroes. It was a magical time, they believed, when fearless warriors fought nightmarish monsters and humans directly interacted with the gods.

Bronze Age Greece

The classical Greeks did not know precisely when the Age of Heroes took place. All they could be sure of was that it happened long before their own time. Using a combination of archaeological finds, ancient literary references, and other tools, modern scholars were able to deduce that the Age of Heroes roughly corresponded with Greece's late Bronze Age, lasting from about 1600 to 1100 BCE. (The name derives from the fact that people then used tools and weapons made of bronze, an alloy of copper and tin.)

During that era the Greek mainland and islands were inhabited by two peoples unfamiliar to the classical Greeks. Mainland Greece was populated by early Greek speakers now referred to as the Mycenaeans (named for the imposing Bronze Age fortress at Mycenae in southeastern Greece). On the large Greek island of Crete and on the nearby Aegean Islands, meanwhile, dwelled the Minoans. They engaged in regular sea trade with Egypt and other lands in the eastern Mediterranean sphere. Evidence indicates that at some point the Mycenaeans conquered the Minoans and took over their merchant fleets and trade routes.

For reasons that are still somewhat unclear, sometime between 1200 and 1100 BCE Greece's thriving Bronze Age civilization collapsed. The fortresses and palaces were abandoned, and record keeping, the arts, reading and writing, and several other facets of civilized society disappeared. The three-century-long period that followed is described by modern experts as ancient Greece's Dark Age.

An Ideal of What People Should Be

During that era, the Greek sphere regressed into a village-centered culture in which most of the residents were poor, illiterate farmers and herders. As the generations wore on, they largely forgot their birthright and heritage and came to identify themselves with the particular island or valley where they lived. These small, often isolated regions became the groundwork for the separate, fiercely independent city-states of classical Greece.

Although the Dark Age Greeks underwent a kind of cultural amnesia about the lost Bronze Age world, some muddled memories of important people, places, and events of that era survived by word of mouth. These disordered fragments steadily took on a life of their own in stories about kingly rulers, daring warriors, and powerful gods and goddesses of the dimly remembered past. In the words of the late noted historian C.M. Bowra, the Greeks "saw in this lost society something heroic and superhuman." It

Ancient Greece (circa 500 BCE)

was a both charming and frightening antique world that "embodied an ideal of what humans should be and do and suffer."[1]

As a new, literate, and far more prosperous society—classical Greece—steadily emerged during the 700s and 600s BCE, its inhabitants inherited the corpus of myths spawned in the Dark Age. In their eyes, they were not merely fascinating and colorful. Those tales were also educational in that they provided models for social, political, and moral values, along with practical wisdom.

Crammed with Supernatural Wonders

Particularly crucial to the classical Greeks were the moral and other lessons they learned from tales involving the *theoi*, or gods. Those stories, Bowra writes, "were delightful in themselves and appealed to all who loved bold actions and gallant gestures." Yet they also "played a considerable part in the education of Greek youth." Understanding the human condition, including human values, was crucial to the Greeks, and they discovered that much could be learned from the traditional myths. These were filled with "the dealings of men with gods and implicitly [entirely] with the worth of human actions and the notion that one should exert oneself to the utmost of one's natural powers." That is, people should, where possible, strive for excellence in all things. The more they could learn about themselves as thinking beings, they reasoned, the more effective such efforts might be, and the myths showed "the place of humans in the universe by telling of their relations with the gods."[2]

Even today the Greek gods and their stories are still both powerful and appealing. In part this is because the Greeks envisioned those deities as having human qualities, including some

---

Hera

Queen of the Olympian gods and the protector of women

---

very human faults and bad habits. Zeus, the leader of the gods, for example, had a roving eye for human females, despite his being married; as a result, his wife, Hera, the protector of women, spent much of her time consumed by fits of jealousy. Such human frailties made the gods distinctly familiar and comprehensible and therefore more accessible to the average person. Also, these superbeings inhabited an extraordinary, legendary world crammed with supernatural wonders, larger-than-life characters, and riveting adventures. As a result, their tales remain endlessly entertaining.

Chapter One

Rulers of the Three Great Realms

Today people often call the vast expanse that includes everything that exists the universe. The classical Greeks called it the cosmos. They envisioned the great cosmic sphere, so to speak, as having three principal and distinct sections, or realms. One, the most immediate and important to them, encompassed the lands in which they and other humans dwelled on the earth's surface. The other two cosmic realms were the underworld, the shadowy world lurking deep beneath their feet, and the sky, or heavens, stretching high overhead.

The Greeks were polytheists, meaning they recognized and worshipped multiple gods. Not surprisingly, therefore, they assumed that each of these cosmic realms must be controlled or overseen by a separate deity. Moreover, like nearly all societies in human history, that of the Greeks was patriarchal, or centered around and run by men. So it is only natural that they viewed those primary cosmic overseers as males.

The Gods at War

In the massive corpus of surviving ancient Greek myths, the rulers of the three great realms were brothers with a shared and quite torturous background. These three gods were the leaders of a divine race the Greeks called the Olympians. They were not the first group of deities to watch over the world, having usurped that power from the first race of gods—the Titans. In charge of the latter was the brutish Cronos. Having deposed his father, the sky god Uranus, he was worried that one or more of his own children might do the same to him. So, as they emerged from the womb of his wife, Rhea, Cronos devoured them whole. This proved the grisly fate of young Demeter, Hera, Hestia, Poseidon, and Hades. Nevertheless, because they were gods they were immortal, so they remained alive for years in their father's monstrous gut.

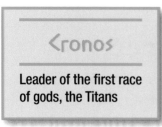

Cronos

Leader of the first race of gods, the Titans

Eventually, Rhea had had enough of this abuse. When she gave birth to her next child, Zeus, she hid him from her husband. Then she wrapped the baby's swaddling clothes around a large rock, and the dim-witted Cronos, assuming the child was inside, swallowed it.

Later, when Zeus was older and strong enough, he decided to challenge his father's authority. He forced Cronos to vomit up the now-grown children he had earlier swallowed. Seething with anger, they joined their brother Zeus in a monumental battle against their pitiless father and most of the other Titans. The Greeks called this enormous conflict the Titanomachy. As the early Greek epic poet Hesiod describes it, Zeus led the attack, "hurling his lightning bolts without pause. The life-giving earth resounded all about with flames and the great forests crackled on all sides with fire. All the earth throbbed with heat. [It was] as if the earth and vast heaven above had come together, so great was the din as the gods opposed one another in strife."³

Zeus

A son of Cronos and the leader of the Olympian gods

After years of devastating struggle, Zeus and his followers were victorious. They became known as the Olympians because they made cloud-wrapped Mt. Olympus, the tallest mountain in

A surviving carved relief shows Rhea holding her son, the infant Zeus. A myth tells how, behind her husband Cronos's back, she had the boy raised in secret on the large island of Crete.

Greece, their home base. Then they set about cleaning up the awful mess the horrific strife had made of the earth's surface. Yet they were well aware that the landmasses of the earth composed only part of the greater cosmos they had won the right to rule. As the late myth teller E.M. Berens worded it, the Olympians now considered how the cosmos "should be divided among them. At last it was settled by lot that Zeus should reign supreme [on the earth], while Hades governed the lower world, and Poseidon had full command over the seas. But the supremacy of Zeus was recognized in all three kingdoms. [He] held his court on the top of Mt. Olympus."[4]

The Olympian Zeus: Wonder of the World

Zeus was such a commanding figure in Greek religion and mythology that the Greeks had many shrines and religious festivals dedicated to him. Of the shrines, the most renowned was the Temple of Olympian Zeus at Olympia (where the ancient Olympic Games were held) in southwestern Greece. Inside the building was an enormous statue of the god fashioned by the Athenian Phidias, who, in later ages, was recognized as the finest sculptor of the ancient world. A few centuries after its creation, the statue was named one the Seven Wonders of the Ancient World. According to the second-century CE Greek traveler Pausanias, who personally visited the temple,

> The god is sitting on a throne. He is made of gold and ivory. There is a wreath on his head like twigs and leaves of olive. In his right hand he is holding a [figure of the goddess] Victory of gold and ivory with a ribbon and a wreath on her head. In the god's left hand is a staff in blossom with every kind of precious metal, and the bird perching on his staff is Zeus's eagle [one of his symbols]. The sandals are gold and so is his cloak, and the cloak is inlaid with animals and flowering lilies. The throne is finely worked with gold and gems, and with ebony and with ivory.

Pausanias, *Guide to Greece*, vol. 2, trans. Peter Levi. New York: Penguin, 1971, pp. 226–27.

Humanity's Savior Sires a Daughter

From that lofty vantage within the swirling clouds that often enveloped Greece's highest peak, mighty Zeus not only oversaw his many fellow deities but also surveyed the wide world of humans. The Greeks believed that he maintained the crucial human areas of justice, law, and morality. They also saw him as a major protector of the hundreds of Greek city-states. (Consisting of a central town supported by a network of surrounding farms and villages, each was, in essence, a tiny nation unto itself. The Greeks did not come together into a unified nation until modern times.) To acknowledge that role, the Greeks sometimes referred to the supreme god as Zeus Polieus, meaning "Zeus of the city." A few of the many other names that described him in his varied roles included Zeus Hikesios, or "Zeus the protector of suppliants"; Zeus Xenios, or "Zeus the protector of strangers"; and Zeus Soter, or "Zeus the Savior."

One might well expect that a god possessing the great stature of Zeus would find his way into a large number of Greek myths, and this was indeed the case. His central place in the stories of Cronos's swallowing the young Olympians and the devastating Titanomachy that followed are but two examples. Another similar tale involving Zeus described how his famous divine daughter Athena came to be. At one point the leader of the gods found himself in a position that mirrored that of his repugnant father. Just as Cronos had swallowed his children out of fear they would overthrow him, Zeus worried that his own future child might pose a threat. The source of

---

Athena

Zeus's daughter and the goddess of war and wisdom

this concern was Gaia, a primitive mother goddess who embodied the earth itself. She predicted that if Zeus had a daughter, she might prove equal to him in wisdom.

To forestall the possibility that he would sire a daughter, Zeus swallowed his first wife, Metis, after she became pregnant. Surely, he reasoned, she could not bear a child while imprisoned in his gut. But he was wrong. Only days after Metis had disappeared down Zeus's gullet, he developed a splitting headache. Normally when used this way, the word *splitting* is only a figure of speech, but this time the metaphor was transformed into reality as the god's head suddenly split open. To the surprise of everyone present, including Zeus himself, out sprang his new daughter—Athena. A deity of war as well as wisdom, she was fully clothed in shining armor, with her invincible breastplate—the aegis—projecting prominently.

The Divine Philanderer

As it turned out, Zeus did not have to worry that his daughter would take his place as the lord of Olympus. In fact, she proved to be his loyal supporter in many instances. Yet Zeus later felt threatened by other deities who dared to question his majestic authority, not least among them Prometheus, one of the few Titans who had fought on the Olympians' side during the terrible Titanomachy.

Although Prometheus initially showed Zeus loyalty, as time went on the headstrong Titan defied his mighty mentor on several occasions. The most serious offense, in Zeus's eyes, was when Prometheus felt pity for the recently created human race, which the Titan had fashioned himself from clay. Prometheus knew that Zeus did not want the humans to gain knowledge of fire, based on the worry that it might make them too strong and independent and thereby less likely to be awed by the gods. Behind Zeus's back, Prometheus stole some fire from Mt. Olympus and gave it to the humans. To punish the disobedient Titan, Zeus ordered him to be chained to a huge boulder on a mountaintop. There, each day, a monstrous vulture devoured the captive's liver, which grew back at night, making the punishment perpetual.

When he was not dealing with threats to his power, Zeus involved himself in all manner of colorful escapades. Perhaps the most renowned of these were his numerous affairs with women—immortals and mortals alike. A majority of these liaisons occurred while he was married to Hera, the queen of the Olympian deities. In fact, although many of the Greek divinities were unfaithful to their spouses, among them Zeus was unarguably the champion philanderer, or husband who frequently cheats on his wife.

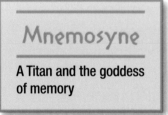

Mnemosyne

A Titan and the goddess of memory

Recounting the stories of all of Zeus's illicit affairs would fill a thick book. Typical was his relationship with the Titan Mnemosyne, the goddess of memory, who bore him nine daughters. These were the famous Muses—protectors and supporters of

An 1897 illustration shows Prometheus chained to a rock, part of his punishment for giving fire to humans. Eventually, the heroic strongman Heracles freed the Titan from this predicament.

the fine arts, who often inspired poets, painters, and musicians. About Zeus, Mnemosyne, and their accomplished offspring, Hesiod writes,

> Zeus entered her holy bed and lay with her nine nights. And when the proper time arrived, the months declined, and the seasons came around and many days were finished, she

gave birth on snowy Olympus, not far from the peak, to nine like-minded daughters, whose one thought is singing and whose hearts are free from care. There on Olympus are their lovely homes, their polished dancing-floors.[5]

Hera was naturally upset about her husband's philandering, and she frequently found herself wracked with jealousy. She occasionally sought revenge against Zeus's lovers, and the case of Semele, the mortal mother of the fertility god Dionysus, shows how cruel Hera's wrath could be. After Zeus impregnated Semele, Hera

Cultural Connections: Poseidon

Large numbers of Greek gods and other mythological characters became so ingrained in Western society that over the centuries they inspired all sorts of literary, artistic, and other cultural works. Poseidon, the ruler of the seas, was no exception. In medieval and early modern times numerous leading painters produced magnificent works depicting the god, sometimes showing him in famous scenes from his myths. (In many cases, they called him by his Roman name, Neptune.) Among these striking paintings are *Mars and Neptune* (1575) by Paolo Veronese and *Neptune Calling the Tempest* (1635) by Peter Paul Rubens. Sculptors, too, captured impressive images of the god, and many of these works still stand in cities across Europe, including Gothenburg, Sweden; Rome, Italy; and Berlin, Germany. Berlin's *Neptune Fountain*, with a splendid carving of Poseidon at its center, is one of that city's main tourist attractions. Even while artists turned out their versions of Poseidon, modern scientists also honored him. Soon after German astronomer Johann Galle observed a new planet—the eighth orbiting the sun—astronomers worldwide agreed to name it Neptune. Later, during the twentieth century, the US Navy decided to name a new rocket weapon it developed the Poseidon missile. Later still, in 2005, novelist Rick Riordan published the first of his hugely popular Percy Jackson books in which that modern young man discovers he is actually Poseidon's son. The first of the series to be made into a major film was *Percy Jackson and the Olympians*, released in 2010.

deceived her husband into displaying his true, blindingly radiant divine form to the young woman, whose body was immediately burned to cinder. At the last minute, Zeus managed to rescue the fetus.

Lord of the Seas and the Earth Shaker

Like Zeus, his brother Poseidon, the leading god of the seas, had many children via multiple lovers. Poseidon's wife, Amphitrite, bore him other ocean deities, including Triton (the messenger of the sea). By other divine mates, Poseidon created a number of giants and other monstrous characters, among them the giants Otus and Ephialtes and the Cyclops (one-eyed giant) Polyphemus, whom the mortal Greek hero Odysseus outwitted and blinded. The latter act naturally angered Poseidon, who punished Odysseus by sinking a raft the man was sailing. Poseidon also sired a number of mortal sons, including the power-hungry kings Pelias and Neleus.

Poseidon, whom the Romans later called Neptune, was famous among the Greeks not only as lord of all earthly waters but also as the so-called Earth Shaker. This epithet, or nickname, derived from the fact that Poseidon caused earthquakes when angry or upset. He was also renowned for one of his symbols—the trident (three-pronged spear), which he carried wherever he went. His other symbols were dolphins and horses.

Among the many myths in which Poseidon figures prominently, several revolve around the famous Trojan War, during which a group of Greek kings laid siege to the rich trading city of Troy in northwestern Anatolia (now Turkey). For various reasons, the sea god came to despise the Trojans. As the Greek epic poet Homer explains in the *Iliad*, about the final year of the war, Poseidon punished Troy's residents by unleashing a giant sea monster on them. The vengeful god also frequently helped the Greeks in their eventually successful siege of the city.

A surviving mosaic from a Roman house in North Africa shows the sea-god Poseidon, whom the Romans called Neptune. He holds his chief symbol—the trident—in his right hand.

In spite of being mainly a sea deity, as the late historian and myth teller Michael Grant points out, "Poseidon claimed a number of lands as specifically his own and quarreled with other gods over them." The best known of these disputes was over Attica, the territory ruled by Athens. Hoping to gain ownership of Attica and get the Athenians to recognize him as their official patron deity, Poseidon got involved in a contest with his niece Athena. Whichever divinity impressed the Athenians the most would be the winner. "Athena created an olive tree," Grant points out, "but all Poseidon could manage to produce was a spring of brackish water where he struck the rock of the Acropolis with his trident. The local people judged Athena's gift the more useful of the two; and to punish them for their choice, Poseidon flooded the surrounding plain of Attica."[6]

The Lord of the Dead

Although Poseidon had failed to gain the role of Athens's special patron, the people of another leading Greek city-state—Corinth—later made him *their* divine protector. In this regard, he did better than his brother Hades. The latter was one of the few major Greek gods who never became the divine patron of a city-state.

The reason is that, as the ruler of the third great realm—the dark and scary underworld—he was widely viewed as a grim, cold, and foreboding character who should be avoided whenever possible. The Greeks did not actually see Hades as evil but rather as a punisher of evil. Therefore, he was not the Greek counterpart of the Christian devil, nor was his subterranean kingdom equivalent to hell. Nevertheless, most people were so wary of him that it was considered unlucky to speak his name aloud. Moreover, no Greeks overtly worshipped him, as they did other gods; this was because he was interested in humans only after they were dead. Indeed, his contact with people was almost always restricted to their shades, or souls.

There were occasional exceptions to this rule, however, primarily when living humans somehow made their way down into the dimly lit underworld and confronted its overlord. One of these brave individuals was the famous Athenian hero Theseus. His friend Pirithous declared that he wanted to descend into the depths and try to rescue and marry Persephone, a beautiful maiden whom Hades held against her will. Theseus reluctantly agreed to help, and the two men traveled deep beneath the earth's surface.

There they found Hades's dismal palace and came face-to-face with the lord of the dead himself. He suspected why they had come and decided to punish them harshly. To fake them out, the great modern myth teller Edith Hamilton writes, "he invited them as a friendly gesture to sit in his presence. They did so on the seat he pointed them to—and there they stayed. They could not arise from it. It was called the Chair of Forgetfulness. Whoever sat on it forgot everything. His mind became a blank and he did not move."[7]

Fortunately for Theseus, the half-divine strongman Heracles (today better known by his Roman name, Hercules) rescued him. Big-hearted Heracles was unable to help poor Pirithous, however. In the timeless corpus of Greek myths, he sits there to this day, silent and unmoving, in Hades's shadowy abode. Pirithous's sad fate stands as mute testimony to the fate of many humans who unwisely challenged the supernatural might of Zeus, Poseidon, or Hades and paid the ultimate price.

Chapter Two

Masters of Nature and the Human Condition

Like other ancient peoples, the Greeks believed that each of nature's wide array of forces and phenomena was caused or guided by one or more gods. Zeus was famous as the master of lightning and thunder, for instance, just as Poseidon was responsible for earthquakes. Also controlled by divine powers, the Greeks believed, were the sun, moon, planets, and other heavenly bodies; the winds; rainbows; volcanic eruptions; the changes of the seasons; animal migrations; and much more.

For the Greeks, therefore, their grand corpus of myths was in part an awe-inspiring and entertaining explanation of how nature works. Yet they were well aware that humanity itself was also part of the natural order. People, the Greeks thought, had been created by the gods in their own image; in this way, people were directly linked both to those deities and to the cosmos from which all had sprung. As Carlos Parada, the author of the *Genealogical Guide to Greek Mythology*, points out, the Greek myths "have connections with all aspects of human life and experience." Often these colorful stories "describe psychological truths; they make emotional valuations and concern themselves with moral, physical or ontological [related to existence] issues; they may convey beliefs, superstitions, rituals, literary images, social ideas, and they may use symbols and allegories as well as reason, philosophy and ethical values."[8] Overall, therefore, the Greek myths frequently describe and comment on the human condition.

The Tragedy of Helios and Phaëthon

In part because the Greeks believed that human traits—both virtues and flaws—reflected those of the gods, many myths describe some aspect of *physical* nature while commenting on *human* nature. Certainly, this was the case with the sun god, Helios, and his best-known myth. The Greeks envisioned him as a strapping charioteer who drove a flaming chariot from east to west across the sky each day. He then returned to the east at night by riding inside a large golden goblet that moved along a river that encircled the earth.

Like several other Greek deities, Helios had slept with mortal women. One of them, Clymene, bore him a human son named Phaëthon. One day, while in a particularly fatherly mood, the god offered to grant the boy whatever wish he desired. Phaëthon, then in his late teens, replied that he wanted to drive his father's luminous chariot across the sky. Initially, Helios was reluctant. According to the ancient Roman poet Ovid, the god explained that his horses were far too powerful for a mere boy to handle. "You seek a privilege that ill befits your growing years," Helios said.

Created in the late 1700s, this carving depicts Helios's son, Phaëthon, desperately trying to control the sun-god's chariot, which careens wildly through the sky.

Helios Honored in Bronze

One of Helios's more important myths explained how he became the divine patron, or national god, of the Greek island city-state of Rhodes (situated off the southwestern coast of Anatolia). Some deities became patrons of cities by winning competitions with other gods, as Athena earned the Athenians' respect by defeating Poseidon in a contest held atop their city's central hill, the Acropolis. Many other deities, however, were assigned by Zeus to become patrons of various Greek cities. When the master of Olympus made that decision, Helios was driving his chariot across the sky, so the sun god missed out. To make up for this oversight, Zeus granted him control of Rhodes. In legend, Helios's three grandsons—Camirus, Lindus, and Ialysus—subsequently ruled the island state and lent their names to its three leading cities.

Later, in around 280 CE, the real Rhodians honored the sun god by erecting an enormous bronze statue of him at the entrance to their main harbor. Dubbed the Colossus of Rhodes, more than a century later the Greek poet Antipater of Sidon chose it as one of the Seven Wonders of the Ancient World. By that time, however, the statue had been toppled by an earthquake. Antipater was still duly impressed, though, because when he visited Rhodes the monument's huge chunks of bronze were still lying where they had fallen decades before.

"Even he whose hand hurls thunderbolts," an obvious reference to Zeus, "may never drive my team."[9]

Nevertheless, Phaëthon kept insisting, and finally his divine father gave in and granted him permission to drive across the sky. No sooner had the young man set out in the chariot, however, when exactly what Helios had feared came to pass. "Lacking now its usual load," Ovid recalls, the gleaming vehicle almost overturned and the alarmed horses "ran wild and left the well-worn highway." Terrified, Phaëthon "could neither use the reins nor find the road." His knees shook and "his eyes were blind with light so bright."[10]

Meanwhile, the galloping steeds ran amok. They yanked the fiery chariot upward, then downward, and every which way; it came so close to the earth's surface that it set entire fields of crops ablaze. The commotion became so great that soon mighty Zeus, then resting atop towering Olympus, felt he must intervene. Hurrying to the scene, he produced a dazzling thunderbolt and hurled it, striking Phaëthon, who was instantly converted into a charred crisp. Both embarrassed and grief-stricken, Helios soon managed to calm his fear-stricken stallions. The sun god had learned the hard way that the all-too-common tendency of human youths toward risky behavior could end in tragedy.

Love Makes the Cosmos Go Round?

Another god who personified a mixture of natural phenomenon and human emotion was Eros, whom the Romans came to call Cupid. Two distinct mythological traditions developed about Eros during ancient times. The oldest, which the poet Hesiod describes in detail in the *Theogony*, pictured this unique deity as one of the first divine beings to appear during the creation of the cosmos. Indeed, well before even the earth itself existed, Hesiod explains, there was only a blurry blob of random elements. The Greeks fittingly called this messy mass Chaos.

Εros

God of love

Eventually, however, two pitch-dark primeval forces came into being—Night and Erebus. In time they gained a semblance of life and became conscious, and although they were simpleminded and crude, they *were* able to reproduce. The great fifth-century BCE playwright Aristophanes described the result of that primitive union, saying "from within the spinning winds inside Erebus's breast appeared an egg." The egg's surface later cracked and out came Eros, the very spirit of love. He displayed "shining gold wings" with which he "flew swiftly through the stormy reaches of the swirling cosmos, and embraced it all, in the process mating with it." While pure white light flooded forth, Eros made possible

The "Sweetest Creature of All"

Eros was said to be irresistibly attractive to women. A description of him as envisioned by the Greeks and Romans appears in the Roman novelist Apuleius's work *The Golden Ass* (in which Eros is called Cupid). The maiden Psyche, who has never seen the god before, approaches his sleeping form and shines an oil lamp on him. She beholds "the gentlest and sweetest creature of all," Apuleius writes, so incredibly handsome that "the lamp's flame quickened in joy." Sinking to her knees, Psyche

> gazed again and again at the beauty of that celestial face, and her spirits revived. She saw the glorious tresses [curls of hair], drenched with ambrosia, on his golden brow, the neatly tied locks straying over his rosy cheeks and milk-white neck, some hanging delicately in front others behind, and the splendour of their shining brilliance made the lamplight dim. Over the winged god's shoulders white plumage glimmered like petals in the morning dew, and though his wings were at rest, soft little feathers at their edges trembled restlessly in wanton play. The rest of his body was smooth and gleaming, such that Venus had no regrets at having borne such a child. At the foot of the bed lay his bow, and his quiver full of arrows, the graceful weapons of the powerful god.

Apuleius, *The Golden Ass*, trans. A.S. Kline, Poetry in Translation, 2013, pp. 76–77. www.poetryintranslation .com.

the emergence of "divine beings, the infinite heavens, the earth, and the oceans' mighty swells."[11]

Somehow the expansive power of love that Eros generated caused the universe's disordered substances to become ordered. Over time that brought about the emergence of the earth and the tremendous variety of nonliving and livings things on it. Eros did not create all these things; rather, he made their creation possible. Thus, in a very real sense the Greeks believed that love was the prime motivating factor of all existence, including the societies of both gods and humans.

An early modern illustration shows the famous mythical lovers Eros and Psyche. Both ancient and modern artists have most often depicted Eros, whom the Romans called Cupid, with wings.

Eros Finds Eternal Love

A later ancient tradition about Eros depicted him as the son of Aphrodite, the goddess of love, and Ares, the god of war. In that well-known scenario, Eros was a supremely attractive young deity whose symbols were a glowing torch and his bow and arrows. In various myths he made humans fall into or out of love, usually by shooting his special benign arrows at their hearts. He was said to be so handsome that most mortal women who gazed on him fell madly in love with him, even if he had not penetrated their hearts with one of his magical arrows.

By far the most famous myth that features Eros in this role of the young, irresistible lover is the one in which he himself falls in love with a beautiful princess named Psyche. She was so attractive, the story went, that Aphrodite grew jealous of her. To vent that emotion, the goddess ordered her son Eros to make the girl fall in love with a gruesome monster.

Eros reluctantly agreed to do his mother's dirty work, but he never followed through. To Eros's surprise, soon after he first saw Psyche, he found that he had fallen deeply in love with her. He expressed that adoration, but only verbally because he refused to allow her to see his true form. One night, however, she quietly approached him while he was sleeping and beheld his striking good looks. When he awoke and realized she had disobeyed him, he was angry and departed in a huff.

Learning about what had occurred, Aphrodite saw another chance to hurt Psyche. The goddess pretended she was helping the girl win Eros back by assigning her a series of difficult tasks that caused her to suffer horribly. Eros eventually realized what was happening and intervened, once again expressing his undying love for Psyche.

Not long afterward, the dashing young god convinced Zeus to make Psyche a demigoddess so that the lovers could remain together always in joy and harmony. Zeus agreed and declared, "I shall declare the union lawful and in keeping with the civil law." He then ordered Hermes to take the girl to towering Olympus. There, the swift-footed guardian of travelers "gave her a cup of ambrosia and said, 'Take this, Psyche, and become immortal. Eros will never part from your embrace [and] this marriage of yours will be eternal.'"[12]

Altered States: Sleep and Death

Two other Greek gods whose actions and attitudes were deeply rooted within both nature and the human condition were brothers, sons of Nyx, the goddess of the nighttime. One was Hypnos, the deity who oversaw sleep. (Words such as *hypnosis* and *hypnotic*, dealing with sleep-like states, derive from his name.) The Greeks believed that he dwelled in a remote cave beneath the Aegean island of Lemnos.

Nyx

Goddess of the nighttime

In his most often cited myth, Hypnos, like many other deities, became involved in the legendary Trojan War. The queen of the gods, Hera, took him aside and requested a favor that only the two of them would ever know about. She explained that her husband, Zeus, had banned her from taking sides in the war. But she desperately desired to aid the Greeks in the conflict, so she urged Hypnos to make her husband go into a deep sleep so he would not realize what she was doing.

Although reluctant at first to risk incurring the wrath of the mighty master of lightning bolts, Hypnos finally agreed to help Hera. The god of sleep caused Zeus to fall into a solid slumber, and Hera leapt into action. At her request, the sea god Poseidon led the Greeks to victory in a battle with the Trojans. Zeus never found out what Hypnos had done, to the latter's good fortune.

Hypnos's brother, Thanatos, also helped humans enter an altered state in which they did not function normally. In Thanatos's case, however, the effect was permanent because he was the god of death. The Greeks did not believe that he *caused* people to die; rather, they saw him as what people today would view as an angel of death who came to take a person to the underworld after he or she died. Greek artists typically portrayed him as an ominous figure who wore a long black robe and carried a sword.

Thanatos

God of death

Thanatos's most memorable myth revolved around his efforts to carry away a young woman named Alcestis, who had bravely offered to die in place of a loved one. Normally no one dared to interfere with him when he was doing his disquieting duty. But on this particular day, the muscular hero Heracles happened to be visiting

Alcestis's family. Determined to keep the menacing Thanatos from reaching her, the strongman lay in wait and, according to the Athenian playwright Euripides, said to himself, "I'll hide there, watch for him, leap out and spring on him; and once I have my arms locked round his bruised ribs, there's no power on earth that will be able to wrench him free, till he gives her up to me!"[13]

When Thanatos arrived, Heracles sprang his trap and the two fought furiously for what seemed like hours. In the end, Heracles won, Alcestis was spared, and the humiliated deity of death crept away into the night. This inspirational outcome seemed to confirm the Greeks' belief that love is the most powerful force in the cosmos.

This splendid painting, completed in the early 1800s by noted Italian artist Pietro Benvenuti, shows the muscular hero Heracles (at left) delivering the rescued Alcestis to her much-relieved husband.

No Second Chances

Not all human heroes in the Greek myths were able to exploit or control nature's divine guardians, however. The story of Odysseus and the god of the winds, Aeolus, is a case in point. Aeolus had initially been born a mortal, but after gaining much favor with the mighty Zeus, he was given the gift of immortality and was placed in charge of the various wind deities. They included Zephryos, who commanded the west wind; Boreas (the north wind); Euros (the east wind); and Notos (the south wind).

Aeolus oversaw them from his palace on a floating island situated in a remote region. One day he received word that a ship bearing Odysseus, the king of the Greek island of Ithaca, had entered the area. Odysseus and his crew had become lost while homeward bound from Troy, which they and other Greeks had besieged and sacked.

Odysseus embarked in a small skiff to meet with Aeolus and then reported back to his men. The god "is willing to aid us," he told them, news that aroused a loud cry of relief and joy. Odysseus explained, "He gave me a bag made of the hide of his own ox and inside he stuffed the winds from all around the area. Aeolus put the bag on my boat and tied it shut with a shiny silver string, making sure that not a single breath of air could escape."[14]

Only the west wind, Odysseus went on, was left out of the bag, so that it could push Odysseus's ships back to Ithaca. For a while this plan, which relied on the men's leaving the bag untouched, worked well and the Greeks made it most of the way home. But then a few members of Odysseus's crew foolishly fiddled with the bag, causing it to burst open and let loose a powerful tempest that carried the ships all the way back to Aeolus's island. There, Odysseus humbly begged the god to offer more help.

But Aeolus now schooled the Ithacans in a harsh reality—that once a human had broken a deity's trust, there were usually no second chances. "Get off my island immediately!" Aeolus told Odysseus. "I for one will not give aid to someone despised by the sacred gods." After showering the man with other angry words, the master of the winds shouted a final "Get out!"[15] and the normally fearless Odysseus beat a hasty retreat.

Inanimate Yet Conscious

In contrast, some nature gods rarely dealt directly with humans; rather, they focused their attentions on fellow divinities. This was the case with most of the Ourea, the very ancient gods who personified the larger mountains. Among them were Athos in Thrace (in extreme northern Greece); Olympus, Helicon, Parnes, and Cithairon (all in central Greece); and Tmolos (across the Aegean in western Anatolia).

> ## Tmolos
> **One of the Ourea and the god of Mt. Tmolos**

To human eyes, the Ourea looked like no more than rocky or forested peaks. Yet each was conscious and, owing to its great age, had the personality of an old man. Each also had physical aspects that symbolized human body parts. Tmolos was an apt example. Ovid describes him as having human-like attributes, including ears, hair, and temples. "On his mountain top the judge was seated," the poet writes. "From his ears he freed the forest trees. Only a wreath of oak fringed his green locks, with acorns dangling round his hollow temples."[16]

In his best-known myth, Tmolos agreed to judge a musical contest between the gods Apollo and Pan. The latter played his famous pipe while Apollo plucked his trusty lyre. Tmolos decided in favor of Apollo, and in Ovid's words, "the sacred mountain's judgment and award pleased all who heard."[17] The images of Tmolos and the other Ourea illustrate how the Greeks endowed even many of nature's inanimate objects with traits that reflected key facets of the human condition.

Chapter Three

Divine Prophets and Healers

The ancient Greek myths are filled with references to prophecy—the foretelling of future events—and to the various means by which such divine predictions are fulfilled. The most direct way in these stories was to consult the gods through oracles—places where people posed questions to those deities. (The priestesses or priests who conveyed the divine answers, as well as the answers themselves, were also called oracles.)

The reason the Greeks had so much interest in knowing what would happen in the future was that they felt inferior to, and frequently feared, the multiple gods they worshipped. The overwhelming power those superbeings wielded seemed to put humans in a precarious position. On the one hand, people offered the deities sacrifices and other forms of worship in hopes of appeasing them. On the other, however, there was almost never any certainty that such worship was enough to win the favor of one or more gods. As historian Charles Freeman puts it,

> The favorable response of the gods could never be guaranteed. It is hardly surprising that there was an intense desire to find out the will of the gods, especially when a choice that offended them might have dreadful consequences. This was the function of the oracles, an attempt to find out the will of the gods before a risky action was taken.[18]

The Greek myths, and Greek society too, also emphasized a special connection between prophecy and healing. This was partly because one of the chief aspects of the future that people wanted to know about was whether a sick person would get better and live or grow sicker and die. Moreover, many of the same temples that contained oracles were also used as the equivalent of modern medical clinics. It was common to bring a sick person to a temple, where he or she rested and slept on the shrine's sacred grounds. The belief was that the local god might communicate with the person through dreams and thereby reveal a cure, a process called incubation. It is not surprising, therefore, that the Olympian god Apollo was seen not only as a master of prophecy but also as a divine healer.

The Renowned Delphic Oracle

In fact, Apollo, the son of Zeus and the Titan Leto, wore many hats, so to speak, in Greek mythology and religion. He was variously called the god of truth; a protector of cattle and sheep; a fighter for good over evil; a champion of the arts, especially poetry and music; and the greatest existing archer.

Apollo's main talent and claim to fame, however, was prophecy—his ability to predict future events. In this regard, the principal outlet for his prophecies was his famous oracle at Delphi in central Greece. It consisted of a beautiful temple, inside of which a special priestess acted as a medium between the god and humans. Over the course of many centuries, rulers, religious pilgrims, and ordinary people alike visited the temple and asked the oracle questions about the future. She usually delivered her answers in wording that was vague, obscure, and open to varying interpretation.

Both the imposing location of the oracle and its many largely reliable predictions made Apollo one of the most exalted and appealing of the Greek gods. The oracle's "very setting," C.M. Bowra

An 1866 colored engraving captures an ancient scene inside Apollo's temple at Delphi. The robed people at left listen to the oracle (with her arms outstretched) as she gives the god's answer to a question they have asked.

points out, "was enough to inspire an awe-struck sense of the god's overpowering presence." The temple was situated "on a ledge under two sheer crags [where] the eye looks down on the plain below, dark green with olive trees and flecked with the shadows of eagles." It is no wonder that the Greeks "believed that through the oracle they were brought into contact with Apollo, and went away comforted and strengthened."[19]

Interactions with Mortals

Although he periodically reached out to humans through his oracle, Apollo also more directly interacted with people from time to time.

One of the chief examples of this appears in some of the myths surrounding Troy and the Trojan War. Apollo, aided by the sea god Poseidon, actually erected Troy's towering walls for the city's king, Laomedon. The latter refused to pay Apollo for the work, however, so the god, who could cause as well as cure illness, released a deadly plague on Troy.

Later, Apollo's temper cooled and he restored good relations with the Trojans. In fact, during their legendary defense of their city against the Greeks, the lord of Delphi sided with Troy's King Priam and helped thwart the Greek siege whenever possible. Apollo unleashed a disease epidemic on the Greek camp, for instance. He also guided the arrow that Troy's Prince Paris shot at the Greek warrior Achilles, striking him in the only vulnerable spot on his body—his heel.

Apollo also interacted with mortals through his affairs with human women. One of them was Coronis, the daughter of a king of Orchomenus in south-central Greece. Apollo fell deeply in love with her the moment he first saw her. Coronis quickly came to feel as strongly for him, and soon she was carrying his child.

The relationship initially seemed like a fairy-tale romance in which all ends well, but unfortunately for the lovers, the opposite occurred. Though well-meaning, Coronis was easily led astray by pretty words. As a result, when a charming young man named Iskhys claimed he loved her more than life itself, she agreed to run away with him. Apollo soon discovered what had happened and flew into a rage. His divine sister Artemis, the goddess of wild animals and hunting, happened to be with him

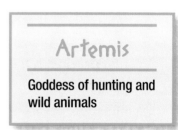

Artemis

Goddess of hunting and wild animals

at the time and offered to punish the unfaithful girl. As skilled with a bow as her brother was, Artemis located Coronis and let loose a flurry of arrows, killing her.

A few days later, Coronis's devastated parents went about the unhappy task of cremating her. They had just put her remains on a pyre when Apollo suddenly had a change of heart.

He "repented of the cruel punishment he had exacted, and hated himself [for] allowing his anger to blaze up in such a way," Ovid writes. Thinking he might still have enough time to save her, he rushed to the pyre. "But he applied his healing arts without avail," Ovid continues. "His aid came too late." At that desperate moment, Apollo remembered the child she was carrying. "That his own seed should perish in those same ashes was more than he could bear. He snatched his son from his mother's womb and saved him from the flames."[20]

A Supremely Caring Individual

When hearing or reading about this myth, average ancient Greeks likely considered that they were rather fortunate that Apollo had managed to save his son from certain death. This is because that child grew up to be Asclepius, the Greek god of medicine and healing. Greeks everywhere admired him, seeing him as a mild-mannered, supremely caring individual who sincerely wanted to heal the sick. Probably for this reason, temples dedicated to him appeared widely in Greece as soon as city-states began to emerge in the wake of the Dark Age. The medical clinics established within those shrines became known as *asclepieia* after his name.

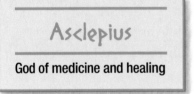

Asclepius

God of medicine and healing

The most often cited myth about Asclepius deals with his supposed ability to raise the dead and the punishment he received for it. According to the first-century BCE Greek historian Diodorus Siculus, the god of medicine

devoted himself to the science of healing and made many discoveries which contribute to the health of mankind. And so far did he advance along the road of fame that, to the amazement of all, he healed many sick whose lives had been despaired of, and for this reason it was believed that

This 1877 oil painting by famed English artist John William Waterhouse depicts a mother holding her sick child in a temple dedicated to the healing god Asclepius. Such temples doubled as medical clinics.

he had brought back to life many who had died. Consequently, the myth goes on to say, Hades brought accusation against Asclepius, charging him before Zeus of acting to the detriment of his own province, for, Hades said, the number of the dead was steadily diminishing, now that men were being healed by Asclepius.[21]

Asclepius professed his innocence and insisted that he was such an effective physician that he was able to save more sick people than anyone before him had. But Zeus accepted Hades's version of events. The master of Olympus immediately slew Asclepius

Apollo's Swift Pursuit of Daphne

One of Apollo's most famous myths recounted his unrequited love for the nymph (minor nature goddess) Daphne. "At one look," the Roman poet Ovid writes, "Apollo loved her. As he gazed, 'Daphne,' he thought, 'is mine.'" This amorous thought turned out to be wishful thinking, however. Daphne was extremely shy and did not have feelings of love for Apollo. Thus, she ran away when he tried to approach her. Moreover, to his surprise and frustration, he found that she could run amazingly fast. He labored hard to try to catch up, but she managed to stay just ahead of him. She maintained "their increasing pace," Ovid recalls, "until his lips breathed at her shoulder." As for Daphne, she worried that the god *would* eventually catch her, so she called out to her father, the Ladon River, for aid. At her request, he transformed her into a laurel tree. When Apollo saw what had happened, he tenderly "embraced the lovely tree whose heart he felt still beating in its side." Filled with sadness, he whispered, "Daphne, who cannot be my wife, must be the seal, the sign of all I own, an immortal leaf entwined in my hair as hers. And by this sign my constant love, my honor shall be shown." This was why Apollo, numerous other deities, and many humans, including victorious athletes, thereafter wore laurel leaves in their hair.

Ovid, *Metamorphoses*, trans. Horace Gregory. New York: New American Library, 1963, pp. 44–46.

with a thunderbolt. (He could die because his mother had been mortal, making him half mortal.) Outraged by this act, Asclepius's father, Apollo, struck back by killing several of the Cyclopes, who were Zeus's sons.

The Old Man of the Sea

In spite of Asclepius's untimely demise, people all over Greece continued to worship him and erect temples in his honor. This was partly because there was a universal respect for and interest in sincere, caring healers. No less compelling to most Greeks were gods possessing prophetic powers, like Apollo. Although the latter was the most-gifted divine prophet mentioned in the myths, a number of other deities could see into the future to one degree or another.

Among these clever characters were several sea gods, including the extremely ancient Nereus. Some surviving accounts say he was even older than Poseidon. For this reason, Nereus,

In this lively 1852 color lithograph, the famous heroic strongman Heracles, whom the Romans called Hercules, wrestles with the sea-god Nereus. In the myth, Heracles wins the fight.

Gaia

The primordial goddess who personified the earth itself

a son of the earth goddess Gaia and the sea deity Pontus, was frequently called by the epithet "the Old Man of the Sea."

Another of Nereus's supposed special talents was the ability to change his shape at will. In one widely popular myth, the heroic strongman Heracles diligently searched for the legendary Garden of the Hesperides (which contained some priceless golden apples). All he knew was that it lay somewhere in the vast ocean encircling the earth's landmasses. Realizing that Nereus had exceptional powers of perception, the hero asked him whether he knew where the garden was. But the shy and reclusive god shied away and tried to hide by assuming the shape of one sea creature after another.

This did not fool Heracles, however. He grabbed hold of the elusive deity and held him fast. Nereus reacted with a display of strength of his own, and the two wrestled vigorously until they were exhausted. Eventually, the aged shape-shifter felt he had no choice but to reveal the location of the garden to his brawny opponent.

Humanity's Daring Father

More renowned than Nereus among the gods possessing prophetic power was the Titan Prometheus, said to be both the wisest of the gods and a true seer. Indeed, his very name meant "forethought." Son of the Titans Iapetus and Themis, Prometheus was well-known for creating the human race from mud or lumps of clay.

Prometheus had an up-and-down relationship with Zeus. At first, the leader of the Olympian gods considered Prometheus a friend and companion, partly because the Titan had backed Zeus during the Titanomachy. So impressed was Zeus with Prometheus's loyalty and wisdom that he made him his most trusted adviser.

Later, however, Zeus began to regret that choice. The troubles started when the leader of the gods asked Prometheus for

Cultural Connections: Prometheus

Prometheus became such a beloved character, not only to the ancients but also to later generations, that Western civilization contains countless cultural references to him and his deeds. Among the earliest was the Athenian playwright Aeschylus's classic 460 BCE play *Prometheus Bound*, which dramatized the Titan's courage in the face of adversity. Other plays about Prometheus, or ones that mentioned him, appeared over the centuries. English playwright William Shakespeare's plays, for instance, are filled with references to that god. One is a line from the comedy *The Merry Wives of Windsor*, in which one character meanly tells another, "Let vultures grip thy guts!" This referred to the vulture that daily tore out Prometheus's liver in the myth about his punishment by Zeus. To the dozens of plays that deal with Prometheus can be added hundreds of paintings by the world's greatest artists. Only a few of those masterworks were those of Peter Paul Rubens (1611), Jan Cossiers (1636), and Louis de Silvestre (1701). A number of great sculptors were also inspired by the courageous Titan. In 1934 noted American sculptor Paul Manship completed the gigantic gilded bronze statue of Prometheus that still flanks the skating rink in the Lower Plaza of Rockefeller Center in New York City. Among other artists who have tackled the god's image or story are filmmakers, including famed director Ridley Scott in the 2012 big-budget movie *Prometheus*. There are even video games about Prometheus, including *God of War II*, released in 2007.

William Shakespeare, *The Merry Wives of Windsor*, act 1, scene 3, line 42.

his opinion about how the recently fashioned humans should go about making animal sacrifices to the gods. In his *Astronomica*, Pseudo-Hyginus (a second-century CE Roman writer whose exact identity is uncertain) told the story, saying in part,

> When the men of old with great ceremony used to carry on the sacrificial rites of the immortal gods, they would burn the victims entire in the flame of the sacrifice. And so, when the poor were prevented from making sacrifices on

account of the great expense, Prometheus, who with his wonderful wisdom is thought to have made men, by his pleading is said to have obtained permission from Zeus for them to cast only a part of the victim into the fire, and to use the rest for their own food.[22]

Zeus agreed to this practice, which became the custom. But Prometheus knew full well that Zeus had plenty to eat and did not need *any* of the meat the mortals offered up to the gods. Because the humans were mostly poor, the Titan worried they might starve. To make certain they got enough to eat, he changed the rules behind Zeus's back. Thereafter, the mortals burned only the bones and fat in their sacrifices and kept all the meat for themselves.

When Zeus found out what had happened, he was livid. As a punishment, he denied the humans knowledge of fire, which meant they could not cook the meat they kept for themselves. Prometheus felt compelled to go behind Zeus's back again, steal fire from Olympus, and secretly give it to the humans. Although the Titan suffered greatly for this offense, Prometheus felt it was worth it. With his power to see into the future, he realized that his small but scrappy creations would retain the use of fire. With it they would cook their food, smelt metals for tools and weapons, and build a mighty civilization. In the fullness of time, they would also cherish the tale of how their daring father had risked all to ensure their lasting success.

Chapter Four

Protectors of Flocks and Fertility

Agriculture was the mainstay of all ancient economies, including that of the Greeks. Most people were farmers who produced their own food by growing crops and/or raising animals, especially sheep, cattle, and goats. Despite fertile soil and good grazing land, starvation was only ever a few bad harvests away. Plentiful rain often kept life in balance, but it was never assured in Greece's hot, semiarid climate. The people knew to expect occasional periods of drought.

To ensure rainfall and other key requirements of the land's productivity, people frequently sought the intervention and favor of appropriate gods. Any deity might be helpful to some degree. But the most supportive ones for farmers and herders were those who specialized in fertility, including Dionysus, who oversaw grape harvests and the soil's richness, and Pan, who protected herders and their flocks. The fourth-century BCE Athenian historian Xenophon emphasized the importance of seeking the aid of those deities, saying,

> ## Dionysus
>
> **God of fertility, grape vines, and wine**

I imagine you are aware that people engaged in war [ask for divine support] and use sacrifices and omens to inquire what they ought and ought not to do before they embark on hostilities. Do you think it is any less necessary to ask the gods for mercy where agricultural affairs are concerned? Sensible farmers, I can assure you, worship and pray to the gods about their fruits, grain, cattle, horses, sheep—yes, and all their property.[23]

The Leading Fertility God

It is not surprising, therefore, that Greek mythology is replete with stories about the fertility gods and people's interactions with them. Chief among these deities was Dionysus, who also oversaw vineyards and wine production. It is interesting to note that his myths grew in number and importance over time, and new stories about him were still appearing during Greece's classical age. The youngest of the Olympian gods, he was only a minor divinity when, during the eighth century BCE, Homer mentioned him briefly in the *Iliad* and the *Odyssey*. But by the third century BCE, he was the most widely worshipped god in the Greek-speaking lands.

The great size of that following was based to some extent on Dionysus's enormous physical appeal. The ancient Greeks envisioned him in literature, paintings, and sculptures as an extremely handsome, somewhat effeminate young man who was an expert at seducing females—immortals and mortals alike. A number of descriptions of that popular image of the god have survived, including a passage from the *Bacchae*, a play by the fifth-century BCE Athenian Euripides. One character says to Dionysus, who also appears in the play, "You have a not unhandsome figure [and] those long curls of yours show that you're no wrestler, as they cascade close over your cheeks, most seductively. Your complexion, too, shows a carefully preserved whiteness. You keep out of the sun and walk in the shade, to use your lovely face for courting [women]."[24]

Partly because his worship became so widespread and peoples of diverse heritages embraced him, Dionysus acquired other names. They included Bacchus, Bromius, Lenaeus (meaning "of the wine vat"), and Dendrites ("of trees"). Similarly, different peoples viewed him in different ways. So, it was thought that he had

The classical Greeks believed that the deity of vines and wine, Dionysus, was uncommonly handsome, yet in a slightly feminine way, as he is depicted (at left) in this nineteenth-century oil painting.

weirdly contrasting sides to his character. Sometimes he was a jovial, tipsy, fun-loving rustic who was the life of the party. Other times he was a mysterious, primitive, and dangerous individual who aroused people's basest and vilest instincts.

A Terrible Realization

Of the many myths associated with Dionysus, the ones that dealt with his more mystical, intimidating, and at times chilling and scary side were the most compelling. One of the best-known tales was also dramatized by Euripides in the *Bacchae*. In addition to

The Golden Touch

Dionysus was famous for his wanderings and adventures in remote areas of Greece as well as in foreign lands. Some of the more distant places he visited included Egypt, Syria, and Phrygia (in Anatolia). Closer to home, Dionysus visited the large Greek island of Crete because one of his followers, Silenus (who had a horse's ears and tail) had become lost and found himself marooned there. Fortunately, the local king, Midas, treated Silenus fairly and fed and housed him, which pleased Dionysus when he arrived to guide Silenus back the Greek mainland. To reward the Cretan ruler, Dionysus told him he could wish for anything he wanted and it would instantly be his. Midas thought it over and then asked Dionysus to make everything he touched turn to pure gold. The god had the wisdom and foresight to realize this would backfire on Midas but granted the request anyway to teach him a lesson. Sure enough, as Midas walked through his palace, he quickly turned tables, chairs, carpets, combs, swords, statues, and all manner of other objects into glittering gold. The man was overjoyed until he sat down to eat dinner and found that his food, too, became a shiny metal at his touch. Realizing he would soon starve to death, Midas begged Dionysus to take back the gift he had granted, and, satisfied the man had learned his lesson, the god did so.

Dionysus, other major characters in the myth were his mortal cousin Pentheus, the king of Thebes; Pentheus's mother, Agaue; and Agaue's father, Cadmus, the founder and first king of Thebes. (Located north of Athens, Thebes was one of Greece's oldest and most important city-states; as a result, a hefty proportion of the stories in the Greek corpus of myths deal with that city and its early rulers.)

In the story, Dionysus, disguised as a human male, paid a visit to Thebes in hopes of gaining new followers. Suspecting the stranger of ill intentions, Pentheus, unaware of the visitor's true identity, had him arrested and thrown into a dungeon. Meanwhile, Agaue and the other royal women journeyed into the countryside to engage in some religious rites.

To avenge himself on Pentheus, the god caused those women to lose their senses and sink into a wild and savage frenzy. When the king heard reports that the women were tearing animals apart with their bare hands and drinking their blood, he hurried out into the wilderness to investigate. Still under Dionysus's malicious influence, the women came upon Pentheus and ripped him limb from limb. His own mother then carried his head back to the Theban court, thinking it was a lion's head.

When Agaue showed the grisly object to Cadmus, he shrank away in horror. Her frenzied spell now wearing off, she could tell by his reaction that something was amiss. "What am I looking at?" she asked in the *Bacchae*. "What am I holding?" As the terrible realization of what she held swept over her, she cried out, "O gods! What horror!" Loudly she shrieked, "It is Pentheus's head I hold in my accursed hand!" When she asked who had killed her son, Cadmus grimly told her the truth. "You killed him," he whispered, "you and your sisters." He added that none of the women realized what they were doing. "You were mad," Cadmus said, because Dionysus had robbed the women, along with many other Thebans, of free will and manipulated their minds. "The whole city was possessed by Dionysus!"[25] Cadmus told her.

The Greeks learned much about the world, and especially about the gods and their fearsome powers, from myths. In this regard, the tale of Dionysus's transformation of the royal Thebans into mindless murderers was one of the most instructive of those stories. It served as a warning to anyone who might dare to challenge or insult one of those divine beings. Euripides summed it up well in a line he gave to Cadmus: "If there be any man who derides [mocks] the unseen world, let him consider the death of Pentheus, and acknowledge the gods."[26]

Pan and the Athenians

Another resident of that unseen world in which the Greek gods roamed also had the power to affect the livelihood and prosperity of humans and their society. Known to the Greeks as Pan, he oversaw and protected shepherds and their flocks and pasture-lands. It was thought that he also watched over wooded groves and other similar quaint natural settings.

The son of the Olympian messenger god, Hermes, Pan was most often depicted in art as having the upper body of a human male and the legs, hooves, ears, and horns of a goat. He almost always bore a musical pipe equipped with multiple reeds, called a

Pan lived in the woodlands rather than on Mt. Olympus. This 1913 illustration shows the pointy-eared divinity playing the famous musical pipe he was credited with inventing.

syrinx, which he was credited with inventing. Today it is frequently called a panpipe in his honor.

Pan did not require that instrument to get people's attention, however. He was said to possess an astoundingly loud voice that could frighten the unwary. During the Gigantomachy, a terrible battle between the gods and a race of giants, his voice startled the giants and created panic and chaos in their ranks. (The word *panic* likely comes from his name.)

Being a rustic god, Pan lived in the wilderness instead of dwelling with his father on Mt. Olympus. As a result, the Greeks rarely worshipped Pan in temples. Rather, most of their sacrifices to him took place in the countryside, especially in wooded areas.

As was the case with Dionysus, some of Pan's myths developed well after Greece emerged from the Dark Age and city-states arose. Indeed, one of the goat-eared god's most charming stories began to circulate in the wake of the first Persian invasion of mainland Greece in 490 BCE. Shortly before the famous Battle of Marathon, in which the Athenians defeated a Persian army, Athenian authorities sent a long-distance runner named Pheidippides to enlist the aid of other Greeks. While on that journey, he passed through a forest and supposedly encountered Pan. The deity informed Pheidippides that he felt neglected by the Greeks. According to the fifth-century BCE Greek historian Herodotus, Pheidippides claimed that the god

> called him by name and told him to ask the Athenians why they paid him no attention, in spite of his friendliness towards them and the fact that he had often been useful to them in the past, and would be so again in the future. The Athenians believed Pheidippides' story, and when their affairs were once more in a prosperous state they built a shrine to Pan under the Acropolis. [Ever since] they have held an annual ceremony, with a torch-race and sacrifices, to court his protection.[27]

Cultural Connections: Pan

Although Pan was not one of the major Olympian gods, the rustic deity of shepherds, flocks, and pastures generated a rich and lively corpus of cultural explorations and references over the centuries. As was the case with several of the Greek divinities, he inspired numerous European painters during the Renaissance. Around 1490, for example, the Italian artist Luca Signorelli painted the *Court of Pan*, which shows Pan sitting on a throne ringed by human worshippers. Later, in about 1506, another Italian master, Cima da Conegliano, produced *The Judgment of Midas*, showing the horned god in the midst of a music competition with the god Apollo. Pan also appeared frequently in early modern literature. Popular English playwright Ben Jonson staged a masque (play-like skit) titled *Pan's Anniversary* at the English royal court in 1620, for instance. Other literary works featuring Pan came during the ensuing centuries, among them Welsh writer Arthur Machen's horror tale *The Great God Pan* (1890), and Scottish writer J.M Barrie's immortal play *Peter Pan* (1904). Barrie based the title character partially on the mythological Pan, describing the boy as part animal and part human. Barrie's underlying aim was to explore human civilization's good and bad qualities. Walt Disney turned the play into an animated film in 1953, with actor Bobby Driscoll supplying Peter's voice. Live-action movies based on Peter Pan appeared in 1991 (*Hook*, with Robin Williams as Peter) and 2003 (*Peter Pan*, with Jeremy Sumpter as Peter).

Up with Gardens; Down with Donkeys

Pan was not the only deity who protected flocks, sheep, and goats. Another was Priapus, who also looked after various fruit trees, gardens, and bees. Not only did he oversee gardens and crops himself, but he also protected them indirectly in the form of artificial versions of himself. Many Greek farmers set up scarecrows among their crops that were purposely fashioned to represent Priapus.

These images were effective because they were scary, which derived from the fact that the Greeks saw Priapus as one of the few divine beings who was born ugly rather than attractive. What made this seem particularly strange was that his mother was none other than the su-

premely beautiful Aphrodite, the goddess of love. (His father was Hermes or Dionysus, depending on which ancient tradition one accepted.) For reasons unknown, the young deity's body was small and badly deformed, including a twisted spine and some unsightly oversized genitals.

Perhaps the most often cited myth about Priapus tells about the unusual circumstances of his birth. "His mother was so horrified at the sight of him," E.M. Berens explained, "that she ordered him to be exposed," or left outside to die, "in the mountains." Luckily for Priapus, however, "he was found by some shepherds, who, taking pity on him, saved his life."[28]

Another mythical tale involving the protector of gardens dealt with his hatred of donkeys. Although outwardly deformed, on the inside Priapus was like most other gods and humans in that he possessed strong emotions, including amorous ones. After developing feelings for the lovely nymph Lotis, one day he noticed her lying fast asleep under a shade tree. He was about to awaken her and express his love when a donkey brayed, jolting her awake. Seeing the misshapen god kneeling beside her, she panicked and ran away. After that, Priapus expressed his dislike of donkeys whenever possible and even went so far as to encourage mortals to slaughter any donkeys they saw.

From Sickly Child to Divine Judge

Whereas Priapus was in charge of gardens and herding animals, Triptolemus oversaw wheat and other grains, including the process in which they were milled using large, heavy circular stones.

Triptolemus was also a teacher of sorts, as he traveled from city to city and region to region and instructed farmers in how to cultivate grain crops. His means of transport was a magical chariot drawn by two winged dragons, like the one the agricultural goddess Demeter drove. Appropriately, considering his talents and duties, his name was based on the Greek words *triptos* and *lemma*, together meaning "he who pounds the grain husks."

Triptolemus was one of several so-called demigods. They were mortals, each of whom was selected by a deity and given various magical or other powers needed to accomplish a given task or job. In fact, one of the chief myths associated with him is the one that explains how he *became* a demigod.

The tale begins with Triptolemus's birth in Attica, the large peninsula of southern Greece controlled by Athens. As a child he was sickly and eventually it looked like he had only a few days to live. By chance, however, kindly Demeter was passing through the village and the boy's father begged her to help his ailing son. The goddess immediately agreed, went to the sick child, and touched her lips to his. According to Ovid in his long poem the *Fasti*, "His pallor [paleness] fled, and sudden strength was visibly imparted to his frame. Such vigor flowed from those lips divine. There was joy in the whole household."[29] Another ancient account claims that Demeter breast-fed the unwell child, who not only recovered but also, infused with her divine milk, transformed into a perfectly formed young man in the course of a few hours.

All versions of the story agree on what happened next, however. Namely, Demeter decided to make Triptolemus her assistant and send him out to spread knowledge of growing and harvesting life-giving grains, which humanity sorely needed. "That boy of

A delicately fashioned image on a ceramic cup dating to around 460 BCE shows Triptolemus (sitting on his dragon-drawn chariot) conferring with his divine mentor, Demeter, goddess of agriculture.

yours," she told his parents in the *Fasti*, "will be the first to plow and sow and reap a great reward from the turned-up soil." After teaching her new protégé what he needed to know, the goddess strode "to her dragons, then soared aloft in her winged chariot."[30]

Many years later, when Triptolemus's vital teaching tasks were completed, Zeus showed his appreciation for a job well done. The master of Olympus made Triptolemus one of the judges of the dead. Most ancient Greeks were comfortable with that because they viewed Triptolemus as a kind, just individual who was sure to judge all who came before him fairly. That he had made it possible for them to reap bountiful crops to stave off starvation was important, to be sure. But no less crucial was the justice he would mete out, for the trait the Greeks most expected from and admired in their gods was a strong sense of justice.

Chapter Five

Heavenly Patrons of Earthly Endeavors

All Greeks, wherever they dwelled, recognized the pantheon of deities headed by Zeus and gave those divine beings respect and worship. Yet in part because there was no overall nation of Greece, but rather a collection of tiny Greek-speaking nations, each of those city-states had its favorite god. In C.M. Bowra's words,

> Every city was protected by its own special deity, who had his or her own temple and festivals. At these festivals, which were still feasts and combined the worship of gods with the gaiety of humans, a whole people might feel that it was protected by watchful presences and united in its admiration for them and its sense of belonging to them.[31]

Ancient Greek religion and society carried this divine protector concept even further. Not only did each city-state have its trusted patron deity, so too did gods watch over various earthly endeavors.

Aristaeus

Protector of beekeepers and overseer of olive growing and cheese making

---

There were divine protectors of a number of common professions, for instance. Hephaestus protected blacksmiths and other craftspeople, Brizo watched over mariners and fishermen. Artemis looked out for hunters, Ares was the champion of soldiers, and Aristaeus protected beekeepers. There were also gods who oversaw people involved with certain aspects of the human condition. As the deity of the human life span, for example, Iapetus protected elderly individuals. Similarly, Charites watched over creative people, Tethys protected nursing mothers, and Hermaphroditus watched over people who today identify as lesbian, gay, bisexual, or transgender.

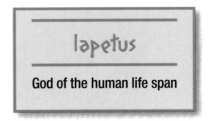

Iapetus

God of the human life span

The Versatile Patron of Travelers

Of the gods who protected professions, among the best known was Hermes, who looked out for merchants as well as travelers of all types. He was also the official messenger for Zeus and the other Olympian deities. In addition, because he was uncommonly versatile, he purportedly invented the lyre (a small harp), astronomy, mathematics, and the alphabet. One of his symbols was the pair of winged sandals he always wore and another was a wooden herald's staff. In keeping with his role as patron of travelers, many Greeks set up small statues of him, appropriately called *herms*, alongside roads to bring good luck to passersby. People also frequently placed herms near the entrances to their houses, convinced that those busts of the god discouraged evil from entering.

Hermes was the product of a love affair between Zeus and the nymph Maia, who was the daughter of the Titan Atlas, who supposedly supported the earth on his mighty back and shoulders. From the start, the young Hermes demonstrated uncanny intelligence and physical abilities, and he proved to be unusually mischievous and prone to pulling pranks on other gods. While still merely a toddler, he swiped fifty cows from Apollo, hid them in a barn, then rushed back to his nursery and played dumb. "I have not seen them," he said, according to the traditional ancient *Homeric Hymn to Hermes*. "I have not heard of them and no man has told me of them. I could not tell you of them, nor win the reward of telling."[32]

Hermes, called Mercury by the Romans, was thought to protect travelers. This nineteenth-century engraving shows him wearing the winged shoes and cap that supposedly carried him swiftly from place to place.

Apollo suspected that Hermes was the guilty party but, for the sake of civility, decided to handle the matter in a friendly manner. Apollo said he would put the lost cattle behind him in exchange for ownership of the lyre, which Hermes had recently invented.

The younger god agreed to the deal, and Apollo suggested they become friends. According to Hermes's hymn,

> Maia's son nodded his head and promised that he would never steal anything of all [that Apollo] possessed, and would never go near his strong house; but Apollo swore to be fellow and friend to Hermes, vowing that he would love no other among the immortals, neither god nor man sprung from Zeus, better than Hermes. And Zeus sent forth an eagle in confirmation [of the new friendship]. And Apollo swore also, "I will make you only to be an omen for the immortals and all alike, trusted and honored by my heart."[33]

After growing into a handsome young god, Hermes took part in many adventures, including some that took place during and shortly after the famous Trojan War. While the conflict raged on, he acted as a diplomat of sorts. Following the killing of the Trojan prince Hector by the Greek warrior Achilles, Hermes saw that Hector's father, Troy's King Priam, strongly desired to bury his son's body. But Achilles refused to hand over the corpse. Hermes intervened and got Achilles to relinquish the body.

After the Greeks sacked Troy, ending the war, Hermes helped the Greek hero Odysseus escape the grasp of the sinister sorceress Circe, who had turned the man's shipmates into pigs. Odysseus decided to go to Circe's residence in hopes of rescuing his men, but suddenly, he recalled (according to Homer), Hermes "came up to me just before I reached the house." The god said, "I suppose you have come here to free your crew, though I think you are more likely to stay with them and never see your home again. However, I am coming to the rescue!" Hermes then "handed me an herb he had plucked from the ground," Odysseus recalled. The god explained that once the man had eaten it, he would be immune to Circe's evil spells. Then the patron of travelers "went off through the island forest, making for Mt. Olympus."[34] Thanks to Hermes, therefore, Odysseus was able to save his men and continue his homeward journey.

The Gods' Chief Craftsperson

Odysseus is hands down the most famous traveler from Greek mythology, so it is only fitting that Hermes, patron god of travelers, would extend him aid in his hour of need. In similar fashion, Hephaestus protected craftspeople of various kinds. In part, this

Hephaestus

Blacksmith of the gods, deity of fire, and patron of craftspeople

was because in ancient times almost all crafts involved some use of fire, including in potter kilns and blacksmith forges—and Hephaestus was the deity who oversaw fire and the forge. Regarding the latter, he controlled the mighty divine forge atop Mt. Olympus and acted as blacksmith to his fellow divinities.

Hephaestus's origins were somewhat mysterious. In some ancient accounts he was the son of Zeus and Hera, but in others Hera gave birth to him miraculously on her own. According to Hesiod, for instance, "Hera, angry, quarreled with her mate [Zeus] and bore, without the act of love, a son, Hephaestus, famous for his workmanship."[35] Evidently, whatever process the queen of Olympus used to produce that child was imperfect because he was born with a lame leg and walked with a limp as a result.

In fact, her son's imperfection greatly upset Hera, and she supposedly used that excuse to toss the child off Olympus and into the Aegean Sea. Fortunately for Hephaestus, the sea goddess Thetis came upon him; during the years that followed, she raised him secretly in a cave. As he grew, he yearned to live where he rightfully belonged—on Olympus—and hatched a plan to make that happen. He learned how to work the forge with tremendous skill and eventually crafted a magnificent golden throne. Then he sent it to his birth mother, Hera, who was delighted with the gift. What she did not realize was that it was designed to entrap her. When she sat on the throne, it held her fast and none of the other gods had any idea how to free her. They needed Hephaestus to do that and invited him to Olympus for that purpose. Once he was there, Zeus admitted it was where he belonged and made him the gods' chief craftsperson, thereby bringing the young deity's plan to full fruition.

Over time, Hephaestus performed numerous services for the Olympians, particularly for Zeus. At the chief god's order, for example, Hephaestus created the first human woman, Pandora. Following another of Zeus's commands, the master of forges

Hephaestus, the divine blacksmith and patron of craftspeople, appears in only a few myths. This sixteenth-century painting depicts the one in which he creates special armor for the mighty Greek warrior Achilles.

crafted a special unbreakable chain intended to hold the Titan Prometheus to a boulder. This was part of Zeus's punishment of Prometheus for giving fire to the recently created humans.

In a related duty, Hephaestus reluctantly led his fellow god to the boulder and shackled him. In the words of the Athenian dramatist Aeschylus, Hephaestus muttered to himself, "How can I find the heart to lay hands on a god of my own race and cruelly clamp him to this bitter, bleak ravine? And yet I must." Then he turned to pitiful Prometheus and with sadness in his voice said,

> With a heart as sore as yours, I now shall fasten you [to] this desolate peak, where you will hear no voice, nor see a human form. But scorched with the sun's flaming rays your skin will lose its bloom of freshness. Glad you will be to see the night cloaking the day with her dark spangled robe and glad again when the sun's warmth scatters the frost at dawn. Each changing hour will bring successive pain to rack your body, and no man yet born will set you free. Your kindness to the human race has earned you this.[36]

The Bringer of Terrible Desolation

The touching, quiet compassion Hephaestus expressed to Prometheus was quite alien to another Olympian who became a patron to humans—Ares, the god of war and protector of soldiers. Greek mythology most often pictured him as a gruff, self-centered ruffian who believed that violence was the solution to nearly every problem. Greek artists, writers, and storytellers depicted him, in E.M. Berens's words, as "a wild ungovernable warrior who passes through the armies like a whirlwind, hurling to the ground the brave and cowardly alike, destroying chariots and helmets, and triumphing over the terrible desolation which he produces."[37]

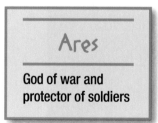

Ares

God of war and protector of soldiers

Ares and the Giants

The sources for the Greek myths about the gods are many and varied. A great many come from poems, especially epic poems like those of Homer and Hesiod. Sometimes a myth about a god was told as a sort of story within a story. A good example is one of Ares's many tales involving his exploits in combat. In this case, the larger myth is the Trojan War, the last year of which Homer chronicled in the *Iliad*. At one point, Zeus is chatting with some goddesses and tells them the story of how Ares once fought against a group of giants who were attacking Mt. Olympus. Two of the giants, Otus and Ephialtes, managed to get the best of the war god, Zeus recalls, and imprisoned him until brave and kindly Hermes found and released his fellow Olympian. According to Zeus (in Homer's words),

> Many of us Olympians have had to make the best of what men do, and we have brought much trouble upon one another. Ares made the best of it, when Otus and Ephialtes made him their prisoner. They shut him up in a brazen jar for thirteen months. Indeed, that would have been the end of Ares the greedy fighter, if their stepmother Eeriboia had not brought the news to Hermes. And Hermes stole him away [from the giants] when he was already in great distress from his cruel prison.

Homer, *Iliad*, trans. W.H.D. Rouse. New York: Signet, 2015, p. 65.

Ares was the son of Zeus and Hera. Not surprisingly, the war god's symbols—a burning torch, a spear, dogs, and vultures—were all connected with military conflict in one way or another. Also, Ares continued the war theme in naming his twin sons—Phobos (meaning "panic") and Deimos ("fear"). The same held true for the war god's daughter, Alcippe, whose name came from Greek words meaning "strong horse." The girl was the product of Ares's affair with a mortal woman named Aglaurus.

Alcippe played a key role in one of Ares's better-known myths. One of the sons of Poseidon raped the young woman, an act that

The Ancient Protectors of Humankind

In addition to individual gods thought to protect various professions and city-states, the Greeks envisioned a group of heavenly beings who protected and bestowed blessings upon humankind as a whole. These were the Daimones (or Daemones), most often pictured in mythology as good-natured spirits. Some dwelled beneath the earth's surface and helped to ensure rich crop harvests; others floated in the air above the earth and sent blessings downward to selected people. According to Hesiod in his epic poem *Works and Days*, these benevolent beings were the descendants of an early, superior race of human-like creatures whom ordinary humans later replaced. The gods, he writes,

> First fashioned a golden race of mortals who lived in the reign of Cronos, king of heaven, and like the gods they lived with happy hearts untouched by work or sorrow. Vile old age never appeared, but always lively-limbed, far from all ills, they feasted happily. Death came to them as sleep, and all good things were theirs. [And] then this race was hidden in the ground. But still they live as spirits of the earth, holy and good; guardians who keep off harm; givers of wealth.

Hesiod, *Works and Days*, in *Hesiod and Theognis*, trans. Dorothea Wender. New York: Penguin, 1987, p. 62.

sent Ares into a blind rage. Methodically, he tracked down and executed the young god with a single swipe of his sturdy bronze sword.

Hearing of his son's demise, Poseidon became as enraged as Ares had been. The sea god knew not to risk attacking a fighter as skilled as Ares, however, and instead resorted to a legal remedy. Poseidon asked all the Olympian deities to meet and try Ares for murder and, if he was convicted, to banish him from Olympus and the earth. The other gods concluded that Ares had been justified in slaying the rapist, so they found him not guilty. Thereafter, the spot where the trial occurred, a low hill only a few hundred feet from Athens's Acropolis, bore the name Areopagus, meaning "Hill of Ares." The classical Athenians held their own murder trials there.

"Incorruptible Beauty and Unfailing Strength"

Even more famous were Ares's exploits on the battlefield. He often won whatever fight he was in, but there were occasional exceptions. The most renowned example took place during the Trojan War, during which Ares supported the Trojans. His stepsister, the war goddess Athena, who backed the Greeks, enlisted the aid of the fantastically skilled Greek warrior Diomedes. She told him to fight Ares and not to be afraid because she would stand beside the man and help him win. In the *Iliad*, Homer describes how Athena "stepped into the chariot beside brilliant Diomedes, and the oaken axle groaned aloud under the weight, carrying the dread goddess and a great man. Athena then took up the whip and the reins, steering first of all straight on against Ares."[38]

Diomedes was one of the finest Greek warriors who fought at Troy. In his principal myth, depicted in this illustration, he rode his chariot straight at the war-god Ares and managed to wound the deity.

Athena made herself invisible, so Ares saw only Diomedes bearing down on him. The war god, Homer writes,

> lunged first over the yoke and the reins of his horses with the bronze spear, furious to take the life from [his opponent]. But the goddess, grey-eyed Athena, in her hand catching the spear pushed it away from the car, so he missed and stabled vainly. After him Diomedes of the great war cry drove forward with the bronze spear; and Athena, leaning in on it, drove it into the depth of [Ares's] belly.[39]

Being a god, Ares was immortal, of course, so the spear thrust did not kill him; it did, however, cause a good deal of pain. First, he experienced the serious physical discomfort of an abdominal wound. The second kind of pain the war god endured was severe humiliation for losing a fight to a mere mortal.

Yet there was little sympathy among the other gods for Ares's loss of face at Troy. They recognized a great truth about themselves and their relationship with humans. Namely those divine beings would live forever, whereas humans—even heroes like Diomedes, Achilles, and Hector—would all eventually die and crumble to dust. This fact, along with the magical powers the gods wielded, made them far stronger and more remarkable than people would ever be. As Bowra so beautifully puts it, the Greek gods

> are able to live as humans would like to live if people were not continually dogged by the morrow [an uncertain future] and the consciousness that at any moment they may pass into nothingness. In their undecaying strength and beauty, the gods have something denied to men, which makes them objects of awe and wonder. The Greek sense of the holy was based much less on a feeling of the goodness of the gods, than in a devout respect for their incorruptible beauty and unfailing strength.[40]

Source Notes

Introduction: The Ideal of What Humans Should Be and Do

1. C.M. Bowra, *The Greek Experience*. New York: Barnes and Noble, 1996, p. 121.
2. Bowra, *The Greek Experience*, pp. 121–22.

Chapter One: Rulers of the Three Great Realms

3. Hesiod, *Theogony*, trans. Rhoda A. Hendricks, in *Classical Gods and Heroes: Myths as Told by the Ancient Authors*. New York: Morrow Quill, 1974, p. 21.
4. E.M Berens, *Myths and Legends of Ancient Greece and Rome*. Wolcott, NY: Scholar's Choice, 2015, p. 20.
5. Hesiod, *Theogony*, in *Hesiod, the Homeric Hymns, and Homerica*, trans. H.G. Evelyn-White. Cambridge, MA: Harvard University Press, 1964, p. 25.
6. Michael Grant and John Hazel, *Who's Who in Classical Mythology*. London: Routledge, 2001, p. 342.
7. Edith Hamilton, *The Greek Way*. New York: Norton, 2017, p. 156.

Chapter Two: Masters of Nature and the Human Condition

8. Carlos Parada, "Basic Aspects of the Greek Myths," Greek Mythology Link, 1997. www.maicar.com.
9. Ovid, *Metamorphoses*, trans. A.D. Melville, in Theoi Greek Mythology, "Phaethon." www.theoi.com.
10. Ovid, *Metamorphoses*, in Theoi Greek Mythology, "Phaethon."
11. Aristophanes, *Birds*, lines 693–95, 698–702, trans. Don Nardo.
12. Apuleius, *The Golden Ass*, trans. P.G. Walsh. New York: Oxford University Press, 1995, p. 113.
13. Euripides, *Alcestis*, in *Euripides: Three Plays*, trans. Philip Vellacott. New York: Penguin, 1974, p. 147.

14. Homer, *Odyssey*, book 10, lines 6–26, trans. Don Nardo.

15. Homer, *Odyssey*, book 10, lines 71–74, trans. Don Nardo.

16. Ovid, *Metamorphoses*, trans. A.D. Melville, excerpted in Theoi Greek Mythology, "Ourea." www.theoi.com.

17. Ovid, *Metamorphoses*, in Theoi Greek Mythology, "Ourea."

Chapter Three: Divine Prophets and Healers

18. Charles Freeman, *The Greek Achievement*. New York: Viking, 2000, p. 139.

19. Bowra, *The Greek Experience*, pp. 60–61.

20. Ovid, *Metamorphoses*, trans. Mary M. Innes. London: Penguin, 2006, pp. 66–67.

21. Diodorus Siculus, *Library of History*, vol. 3, trans. Charles H. Oldfather. Cambridge, MA: Harvard University Press, 1954, pp. 43, 45.

22. Pseudo-Hyginus, *Astronomica*, trans. Michael Grant, in Theoi Greek Mythology, "Prometheus." www.theoi.com.

Chapter Four: Protectors of Flocks and Fertility

23. Xenophon, *The Estate-Manager*, trans. Hugh Reddinick and Robin Waterfield, in *Xenophon: Conversations with Socrates*. New York: Penguin, 1990, pp. 307–308.

24. Euripides, *Bacchae*, trans. Philip Vellacott. New York: Penguin, 1973, pp. 194–95.

25. Euripides, *Bacchae*, p. 222.

26. Euripides, *Bacchae*, p. 223.

27. Herodotus, *Histories*, trans. Aubrey de Sélincourt. New York: Penguin, 1980, p. 425.

28. Berens, *Myths and Legends of Ancient Greece and Rome*, p. 176.

29. Ovid, *Fasti*, trans. James G. Frazer. Cambridge, MA: Harvard University Press, 1959, p. 229.

30. Ovid, *Fasti*, p. 231.

Chapter Five: Heavenly Patrons of Earthly Endeavors

31. Bowra, *The Greek Experience*, p. 69.

32. Hugh G. Evelyn-White, trans., *Homeric Hymn to Hermes*, in *Hesiod, the Homeric Hymns, and Homerica*. Cambridge, MA: Harvard University Press, 1982, pp. 389, 391.

33. Evelyn-White, *Homeric Hymn to Hermes*, p. 401.
34. Homer, *Odyssey*, trans. E.V. Rieu. New York: Penguin, 2006, pp. 163–64.
35. Hesiod, *Theogony*, in Dorothea Wender, trans., *Hesiod and Theognis*. New York: Penguin, 1982, p. 53.
36. Aeschylus, *Prometheus Bound*, trans. Philip Vellacott, in *Aeschylus: "Prometheus Bound," "The Suppliants," "Seven Against Thebes," "The Persians."* New York: Penguin, 1986, p. 21.
37. Berens, *Myths and Legends of Ancient Greece and Rome*, p. 112.
38. Homer, *Iliad*, trans. Richmond Lattimore. Chicago: University of Chicago Press, 2011, p. 150.
39. Homer, *Iliad*, Lattimore translation, p. 151.
40. Bowra, *The Greek Experience*, p. 57.

The Ancient Myth Tellers

Aeschylus

Today often called the world's first great playwright, he was born around 525 BCE. In 490 BCE, when in his thirties, he fought in the pivotal battles of Marathon and Salamis, both against Persian invaders. All of his more than eighty plays (seven of which survive) were heavily influenced by the huge corpus of old Greek myths, parts of which he dramatized in those works.

Euripides

Born in about 485 BCE, this Athenian master of tragic drama wrote more than eighty plays, nineteen of which have survived. He was known for his frequent emphasis of themes and ideas that questioned traditional religious and social values. Among his works that retell important Greek myths are *Alcestis* (438 BCE), *Medea* (431), *Electra* (ca. 413–417), and *Helen* (412).

Herodotus

Often considered the father of history because he wrote the first-known modern-style history text, he was born around 484 BCE. Although he dealt largely with historical events, his book mentions or summarizes a number of old Greek myths. They include episodes and characters from the Trojan War, Theseus and the Minotaur, and Zeus's disguising himself as a bull.

Hesiod

Born sometime during the early 700s BCE, the ancient Greeks considered him one of the two greatest epic poets (the other being Homer). Hesiod was a farmer by trade but devoted much of his time to writing. His two epic poems, *Works and Days* and the *Theogony*, contain a wealth of detail about the early Greek creation myths, including the rise of the first race of gods, the Titans.

Homer

His birth year is unknown, but he likely lived during the 700s BCE. One of several storytellers, called bards, who recited long narratives in public, it appears that he created the final versions of the already existing epics the *Iliad* and the *Odyssey*. For the Greeks, these works, containing many dozens of myths large and small, were crucial sources of their moral codes and social and political attitudes.

Ovid

Publius Ovidius Naso (43 BCE–17 CE), popularly known as Ovid, was one of Rome's finest poets. One of his books, titled the *Metamorphoses*, contains his own retellings of a majority of the important ancient Greek myths. This collection of tales survived Rome's fall and became more popular than ever during medieval times and the early modern era.

Plutarch

A pivotal and widely popular Greek biographer and moralist, he was born in about 46 CE. He is best known for two massive literary works—*Parallel Lives*, consisting of fifty detailed biographies of well-known Greek and Roman military and political figures, and *Moralia*, a collection of absorbing essays on moral, political, philosophical, and other issues. Both works feature references to the traditional Greek myths.

Pseudo-Apollodorus

His real name is unknown and modern experts call him Pseudo-Apollodorus, meaning the "fake Apollodorus." Whoever he was, he likely lived during the first century CE or somewhat later. What is more certain is that his masterwork, often called the *Bibliotheca*, or *Library*, is the largest single compilation of Greek myths penned in the ancient world. If this work had not survived, numerous Greek myths would have been tragically lost to humanity and today be unknown.

For Further Research

Books

Mike Clayton, *Greek Mythology: A Captivating Guide to the Ancient Gods, Goddesses, Heroes, and Monsters*. Charleston, SC: Amazon Digitial Services, 2017.

Edith Hamilton, *Mythology*. New York: Grand Central, 2011.

Sarah Maquire, *In the Beginning Was Chaos: Greek Myths of the Gods and Creation*. New York: Amazon Digital Services, 2015.

Mark P.O. Morford and Robert J. Lenardon, *Classical Mythology*. New York: Oxford University Press, 2010.

Liam Saxon, *A Smart Kids Guide to Ancient Greek Gods and Goddesses*. New York: Create Space, 2015.

Katerina Servi, *Greek Mythology: Gods & Heroes: The Trojan War and the "Odyssey."* Baton Rouge, LA: Third Millennium, 2018.

Internet Sources

Mike Belmont, "The Greek God Hephaestus," Gods-and-Monsters.com. www.gods-and-monsters.com.

Mike Belmont, "Poseidon, Greek God of the Sea." Gods-and-Monsters.com. www.gods-and-monsters.com.

John Black, "Greek Mythology and Human Origins," Ancient Origins, January 30, 2013. www.ancient-origins.net.

N.S. Gill, "Prometheus: Fire Bringer and Philanthropist," ThoughtCo., March 6, 2017. http://ancienthistory.about.com.

Manfred Korfmann, "Was There a Trojan War?," *Archaeology*, vol. 57, no. 3, May/June 2004. http://archive.archaeology.org.

Nick Romeo, "The Gods of Olympus," *Christian Science Monitor*, March 12, 2014. www.csmonitor.com.

Greek Mythology Link (www.maicar.com). This well-thought-out site has a biographical dictionary with more than six thousand entries and some forty-five hundred photos, drawings, and other images.

Mythweb Encyclopedia of Greek Mythology (www.mythweb .com/encyc). Although not as comprehensive and detailed as Theoi (see below), this website provides a lot of useful information about both major and minor Greek mythological characters.

Theoi Greek Mythology (www.theoi.com). This is the most comprehensive and reliable general website about Greek mythology on the Internet. It features hundreds of separate pages filled with detailed, accurate information as well as numerous primary sources and reproductions of ancient paintings and mosaics.

Index

Picture Credits

Cover: vukkostic/iStockphoto.com

8: Maury Aaseng

13: Plaque Campana, Dance of the Curetes, from Myrina, Asia Minor (terracotta) (b/w photo), Greek/Louvre, Paris, France/Alinari/Bridgeman Images

17: ZU_09/iStockphoto.com

20: Triumph of Neptune, pavement from the House of Wadi Blibane, Sousse (ancient Hadrumetum) (mosaic), Roman, (3rd century AD)/Musee Archeologique, Sousse, Tunisia/Bridgeman Images

24: Fall of Phaeton, Wedgwood, c.1785 (jasper), English School, (18th century)/Lady Lever Art Gallery, National Museums Liverpool/Bridgeman Images

28: duncan1890/iStockphoto.com

31: Hercules leading resuscitated Alcestis to her husband Admetus, by Pietro Benvenuti, 1817–1829, fresco/De Agostini Picture Library/Bardazzi /Bridgeman Images

36: Ancient Greece: Shrine to Apollo: The Oracle at Delphi, 1866 (coloured engraving), Leutemann, Heinrich (1824–1905)/Private Collection/© Bianchetti/Leemage/ Bridgeman Images

39: The Visit of a Sick Child to the Temple of Aesculapius, 1877 (oil on canvas), Waterhouse, John William (1849–1917)/Private Collection/Photo © The Fine Art Society, London, UK/Bridgeman Images

41: Hercules and the Old Man of the Sea, illustration from 'A Wonder-Book for Girls and Boys' by Nathanial Hawthorne, 1852 (colour litho), Crane, Walter (1845–1915)/ Private Collection/The Stapleton Collection/Bridgeman Images

47: Bacchus and Ariadne, by Nicola Carta, Detail/De Agostini Picture Library/A. Dagli Orti/Bridgeman Images

50: Sweet, piercing sweet was the music of Pan's pipe, illustration from 'The Story of Greece' by Mary Macgregor, 1st edition, 1913 (colour print), Crane, Walter (1845–1915)/Private Collection/The Stapleton Collection/Bridgeman Images

55: Italy, Val Trebbia, Spina, Detail of a scene of Eleusinian cult, Triptolemus on a winged chariot and Demeter form red-figure Attic krater, painted by the painter of the Niobides, 460 B.C./De Agostini Picture Library/A. Dagli Orti/Bridgeman Images

58: Hermes (engraving), English School, (19th century)/Private Collection/Look and Learn/Illustrated Papers Collection/Bridgeman Images

61: Hephaestus (Vulcan) forging Achiles' weapons, The Trojan Horse, Chamber of Troy (Sala di Troia), 1538–1539, Romano, Giulio (1492–1546) (and workshop)/Palazzo Ducale & Museo, Mantua, Lombardy, Italy/Ghigo Roli/Bridgeman Images

65: whitemay/iStockphoto.com

About the Author

Classical historian and award-winning author Don Nardo has written numerous acclaimed volumes about ancient civilizations and peoples. They include more than two dozen overviews of the mythologies of the Sumerians, Babylonians, Egyptians, Greeks, Romans, Persians, Celts, and others. Nardo, who also composes and arranges orchestral music, lives with his wife, Christine, in Massachusetts.